A Second Basket of Crumbs

A Second Basket of Crumbs

by

T. W. Willingham

Beacon Hill Press of Kansas City
Kansas City, Missouri

First Printing, 1975
ISBN: 0-8341-0345-1
Printed in the United States of America

Contents

It is not a malicious doing but a gradual
neglect that leads to the tragic end.

He Was Gone

In the twentieth chapter of First Kings, a story is told of a man in whose care another had been placed for safe-keeping, and a severe penalty was to be inflicted should he allow the man to escape. He did escape, and the excuse was, "And as thy servant was busy here and there, he was gone" (v. 40).

This incident illustrates well the way by which the Holy Spirit can slip away from our lives. Perhaps seldom is the Spirit deliberately driven from our hearts. The more common way is by neglect, and that is not purposeful. "As thy servant was busy"—that sounds very justifiable. He was not lazy—far from it. He was a pusher—energetic —creative—fully occupied. The only problem was that he was busy with other things than the assigned task—busy "here and there." He was in almost everything. If work could have saved him, he would have been well saved.

One cannot possibly do all that could be done; work is endless. It may be good work—work that represents God's kingdom—but selection has to be made, for all cannot be done. So it is a case of proper assessment of values. What is good, and what is best?

Calls come from every side—good things to be done— Kingdom services to be rendered—but what is of prime importance? When that is decided, then the whole of life should bow to it; when the most important is cared for, the less important will suffer, if anything does.

Activity has been crowned as a cardinal virtue, but

activity—even in good things—may become the very cause of our downfall. Activity is something of us—our effort—our life in expression. The all-important thing in our lives is not so much what we do, but what is done through us.

Here the emphasis is on relationship, and relationship with another means contact, and contact requires time, and time runs out. The day soon closes and the main thing may have been crowded out. This was the case in the story of our subject. Time was gone, and so was the man left in his care.

More than once, we have been warned of the danger of losing the Spirit from our lives. Jesus tells us of the cares of this life and the deceitfulness of riches that choke the operation of the Spirit. In His parable of the sower, it was the crowding weeds that choked out the life of His hearers.

Again, we are exhorted to take heed lest at any time we should let the Word slip away.

The danger here is that one allows his spiritual life to slip away so gradually that its going is almost imperceptible. It is not a malicious doing but a gradual neglect that leads to the tragic end.

The loss of the Spirit comes with the loss of contact with Him; Joseph and Mary's losing the Christ illustrates this. Never did they say to the Son, "Be gone." In fact, they assumed that He was in the company. It was assumed, and yet they had not heard His voice all day. They presumed but did not commune with Him.

Labor seems so justifiable, especially when it is in the cause of God. It has its place, but not the first place. One's first obligation is to a personal God. He's of more value than His work among men. He existed long before man was ever created.

"Here and there" might indicate aimlessness—nothing special in mind—just miscellaneous matters—no real dynamic purpose—and certainly inattention to the matter on which one's life depends. There is no substitute for the primary. The first must be made first, or all of life goes awry.

To the grain farmer, the sowing season is the important one. It matters not how much else he may have to do, if he fails to get his wheat in during the planting season, there will be no harvest. There is only one time to catch a plane, and that is before it leaves the ground.

"I was busy" is no excuse for leaving the all-important task undone. The life depends upon the heart; all of the rest of the body is of no value when the heart is gone.

One must not fail to recognize that one of the enemy's choice weapons to defeat us in the Christian life is to keep us busy—too busy to pray—too busy to think of things divine—too busy to be alone with the One we are to keep.

It must have been a tragic awakening when it was discovered that the escape had been made. Little time and thought had been given to this sacred trust until it was too late. "He was gone." Gone where? That was the question that could not be answered.

Next, the awful penalty was looming before him. There was no escape from it. When one begins to apply this story to one's own life, the matter becomes serious. The frightening ending of the story should put us on our guard. We have been enjoined to examine ourselves to see if we be in the faith, and that advice was never more important than here.

Joseph and Mary's loss of Jesus at first frightens us. Could He be gone all day and they not know it?—only if it could be said that they had held no conversation with Him.

So it is with the Guest of our souls—the Spirit. We need not be in doubt about His leaving if we hold communion with Him. If we have had no conscious contact with Him recently, we should begin the search. He may be recoverable, but the longer the separation, the less likely the recovery. Only if our fellowship is kept up to date can we be sure.

He is the Truth; and when we take the path of truth, we take the path of fellowship with Him.

Growing Up by Speaking the Truth

The Apostle Paul points the way to spiritual growth: "But speaking the truth in love, [you] may grow up into him in all things, which is the head, even Christ" (Eph. 4:15).

The Christian life begins by speaking the truth. The sinner has sins that separate him from God. He must begin by speaking the truth concerning them. He must admit that they are his own, and that he is responsible for them. He must not charge others with his sins. He must be truthful and own them as his own. This is the opening door into life.

One must then speak the truth as to his sinful nature. He must not seek to hide it or condone it. He must not seek to appear to be able to master it. He must admit himself helpless to conquer and expel it. He must be truthful about it. This opens the door for the Cleanser to come in and rid him of it.

One must speak the truth about his faults and weaknesses. He must not try to appear to be what he is not. He must confess—be honest about—his faults. This opens the door for progress in his own life and gives hope to others who are thus afflicted and feel that they are thus alone. One's honesty here helps others to have hope and honesty. Thus growth begins in oneself and in others.

One must speak the truth in his dealings with men.

A Christian's word should be as good as his bond. When another hears him speak, that person should have confidence that he has heard the matter as it is.

He should speak the truth about his fellowman. He must not color the report or deny any part of it. He should deal with others as he would have them deal with him. He should scatter no damaging report that he does not know to be true, and only tell it at all when a good cause may be abetted.

He should tell the truth about his relationship with his God. He should not claim to be living on the mountain heights of Christian living when he actually spends much time in the valley. He should not deny his trials nor the chastening of the Lord.

He should speak the truth about his understanding of God's Word and his lack of understanding. He should not seek to appear to be what he knows he is not. He should not hide an aching heart beneath a coat of smiles in order that his true self may not be known to others. The fact is that to know the trials of others gives hope and courage to us. Thereby we know that we are not alone—someone else understands.

He should be truthful in dealing with others. He must not "polish the apple" for personal gain or say behind one's back what he dare not say to his face. He should say what he means, and mean what he says.

Paul recommends such a course as a means of growing up. How could one grow in grace and be untrue to truth? It is only as one is deeply honest that he may expect to grow spiritually.

Among other things, Jesus said, "I am the truth," and only the truthful can be one with Him.

It is needless to say that to be true to truth is to suffer. Christ was the world's greatest Sufferer. He suffered for what He said, but He spoke only the truth. Paul realized this fact, and asked one of his churches, "Am I . . . become your enemy, because I tell you the truth?" (Gal. 4:16).

Many do not love the truth. They do not want to hear it. It reveals their true, wicked selves and they do not want to be exposed. Jesus had problems with those who opposed the truth, but He himself was always true to truth.

Paul said, "We can do nothing against the truth, but for the truth" (2 Cor. 13:8). Truth is of God, and God cannot be defeated. Truth will stand the shocks of time and the light of the judgment.

One who dedicates his life to the truth must know of a surety that he thereby exposes himself to suffering. For this reason, many shun the truth; but no one but a truth teller and a truth lover can inherit eternal life.

The road to truth is the road upward, and only by traveling this route can the saint grow in grace and in the knowledge of the truth.

Jesus said that the Father sought such as would worship Him in truth. So important is truth that the sainted John wrote, "I rejoiced greatly that I found of thy children walking in truth" (2 John 4). In his third letter he said, "I have no greater joy than to hear that my children walk in truth" (v. 4).

Truth brings freedom, and freedom lends to growth. "Ye shall know the truth, and the truth shall make you free." To know "the truth as it is in Jesus" is to know Jesus. He is the Truth; and when we take the path of truth, we take the path of fellowship with Him toward our eternal home.

"His truth shall be thy shield," wrote the sweet singer of Israel. The wise man urged, "Buy the truth, and sell it not." In the end, the ages must bow at the shrine of truth. It will survive all of life's tempests and stand stalwart and erect amid the wreckage of all that is false.

"Truth, crushed to the earth, shall rise again." It has

13

the strength of the resurrection in it. No wonder the Psalm-ist said, "I have chosen the way of truth." It is the "way everlasting." To speak it is to grow; to live it is to flourish; to deny it is to deny oneself and one's God.

Growth—progress—life—and eternal happiness crown the head of Truth. Her purifying influences sweeten the soul and her energizing power lifts the life above the miasmas of sin, and her redeeming virtue will save our souls. "I am . . . the truth," said the Saviour.

*If Jesus had not dealt with truth, He could
have had more friends, but not more saints.*

Love Produces Enemies

When one affirms, as I now do, that "love produces enemies," he appears to fly into the teeth of truth. Does not love produce love? Do we not "love him, because he first loved us"? Isn't love the winning force of our faith?

Without denying any of these statements, let us look at the other part of the paradox. When we affirm that "for my love they are my adversaries," we affirm a truth. It is in the Word (Ps. 109:4).

This passage does not stand alone. It has a New Testament counterpart. Said Paul, "The more abundantly I love you, the less I be loved" (2 Cor. 12:15).

Let us cement these two biblical statements together by the blood of Christ, and our foundation will then be sure. Did ever man love like Jesus? Did ever man speak the truth in love more fully and more clearly than He? Was ever man hated more hotly than He? Was it not love expressing itself in truth that made His bitterest enemies?

We must reaffirm our theme, "Love produces enemies." To fail to see this is to fail to understand love. Love is truth in action. Many do not care to hear the truth, and when they do hear it, they resent it and hate the teller.

We might also say that truth is love in action; for, in fact, they must go hand in hand. To love is to be true, and to be true is to love.

Was it not love that caused John the Baptist to rebuke Herod, and did not that cost him his head? What caused the prophets to suffer and many of them to die? Was it not love in action?—truth going forth?

The record is that "all that will live godly in Christ Jesus shall suffer persecution" (2 Tim. 3:12). Jesus said, "If the world hate you, ye know that it hated me before it hated you" (John 15:18). We know they hated Him.

Love rebukes, corrects, and warns. Such expressions of love hurt, and at times the sufferer retaliates and hates. There is no way to reprove without hurting, or at least God hasn't found it; for it is said, "Whom the Lord loveth he chasteneth," and, "No chastening for the present seemeth to be joyous, but grievous" (Heb. 12:11).

It would seem that our love seldom develops to the point where it deals in truth that hurts. Perhaps the reason for that is that one knows that, if he thus loves, he may be called upon to suffer, and he prefers not to suffer— hence he dwarfs his love for both man and God. His self-love predominates.

If this line of truth puts the servant of God in the role of a sufferer, we answer that this is the role in which God places him. In the light of this, Paul exhorted young Timothy to "endure hardness as a good soldier of Jesus Christ." A soldier is supposed to be exposed to hurt and even death; so is the soldier of the Cross.

Love divides homes. Jesus makes that crystal-clear: "Think not that I am come to send peace on earth. . . . I am come to set a . . . daughter against her mother" (Matt. 10:34-35).

The lover—the real lover of God and souls—goes out to get each and every one he can for the Kingdom. To be true, he must remind each that, if he is to follow Christ, he must hate (love less) mother, wife, children, and his own life. He must follow Christ, even if his wife turns against him and leaves him. When love makes these scriptural demands and individuals begin to accept the terms and follow the Christ, those left behind may well (and often do) hate the lover who caused this division.

If this seems to be cruel—this splitting homes for Christ—the answer is that it is better to split one from a home and get him to heaven than to leave the home united on its way to hell. Love that demands and accepts such dedication is hard to find; hence, "Many will say to me in that day, Lord, Lord. . . . And then will I profess unto them, I never knew you: depart from me" (Matt. 7: 22-23).

Love demands that the lover require complete consecration of all who would follow him. Such is the demand of Jesus. This could, and sometimes does, mean to answer a call to the ministry or mission field, the giving of large sums of money, or making other sacrifices. Members of the family may object and hate the one who induced their loved one to make such sacrifice.

Love has courage to stand for truth and right, to expose hypocrisy, to rebuke pretense, and to unmask sham and unreality. Jesus produced some of His greatest enemies in this field.

The sham of the Pharisees—their self-seeking, widow-robbing, long-praying-to-be-seen, legalistic rules, and self-righteousness—drew His most scathing denunciations. But He spoke to them in love, and this expression of love made Him bitter enemies. If He had not dealt with truth, He could have made more friends, but not more saints. He chose to love and not be loved, rather than to be unloving and untrue. He could say, "For my love they are my adversaries." It runs this way.

The challenge of the "ifs" can be measured only by the grandeur of the promises that follow them.

The Disturbing "Ifs"

There are more than 1,500 *ifs* in the Word of God. On some of these two-letter words hang eternal destinies. Some of them are disturbing. As a rule, they are both challenging and disturbing.

Since we have all sinned and must be forgiven or else be lost, we should probably head the list with "If we confess our sins, he is faithful and just to forgive us our sins" (1 John 1:9).

This is a wonderful promise—just the one that we need. But it is not absolute—only conditional. Its fulfillment does not rest upon an unfailing God but upon the act of a free moral agent over whose will God has no final control.

Now comes the *if* of fellowship. What a wonderful way to live—in fellowship with the Father and His Son! Paul tells us that we are "called unto the fellowship of his Son." But here again we meet the conditional *if:* "If we walk in the light . . . we have fellowship" (1 John 1:7). Here again we are thrown back upon ourselves, for fellowship is not guaranteed, and one may walk the whole journey of life without it.

The forgiveness of our trespasses is promised: "Your heavenly Father will also forgive [your trespasses]." This is a most wonderful promise, but like the others, it hinges upon our act: "If ye forgive men their trespasses" (Matt. 6:14). Nothing is guaranteed here except on conditions to be met by us.

One of the most astounding promises of God is "Ye shall ask what ye will, and it shall be done unto you" (John 15:7). Who will dare to pare this promise down to fit his prayer life? It must stand, if Christ can stand, and stand as spoken—"Ask what ye will, and it shall be done." Fantastic? Colossal? Yes, but true, for Christ said it. But He protected it by: "If ye abide in me, and my words abide in you." Here again Jesus might have well said, "But go ye and learn what that meaneth." It challenges our deepest thought. Can we meet the challenge of its *if?* It haunts me.

Achieving faith has ever been a challenging goal. A climactic promise here is found in Jesus' words, "Nothing shall be impossible unto you" (Matt. 17:20). The anchor to which this limitless promise is tied is "If ye have faith as a grain of mustard seed." Here again the onus is on us— the measure of our faith.

"Ye shall abide in my love" (John 15:10). What an abiding peace! Can it be ours? Yes, and on this condition: "If ye keep my commandments."

"We are made partakers of Christ" (Heb. 3:14). What a glorious promise! The same writer affirms that "God dealeth with you as with sons" (12:7). But both of these promises depend upon us for their fulfillment. The disturbing *if* hovers over them. To realize them one must "endure [the] chastening [of] God" and we must "hold the beginning of our confidence stedfast unto the end." The burden still rests with us. We determine the outcome. God only makes it possible; it is for us to make it actual. The *if* opens or closes the door.

God has built us for a "temple of the Holy Ghost" (1 Cor. 6:19), but we can keep this Guest only "if we hold fast the confidence and the rejoicing of the hope firm unto the end" (Heb. 3:6). Here again the *if* meets us.

The honor of high heaven is promised us: "Him will

my Father honour" (John 12:26). But this honor is conditioned on "If any man serve me."

A bountiful harvest is promised: "In due season we shall reap" (Gal. 6:9). That is most encouraging, for there are times when it seems that the sowing is the only service. But here the harvest is promised. Yes, that is, "if we faint not."

Perhaps the most wonderful promise to be fulfilled this side the grave is "Ye shall never fall" (2 Pet. 1:10). There has been much trafficking in this promise, and in many instances it has been sold short. It has been divorced from its setting and those who have thus divorced it may be in that "many" who will hear the shocking words "Depart . . . I never knew you." This glorious promise has been safely guarded: "If ye do these things"—things clearly stated—then "ye shall never fall."

We come now to the great divide—the line that marks the end of time for us. Here it is thrilling to note that the promises govern the end and even extend into the eternities.

The resurrection in Christ is promised. All will be raised, but only those in Christ will be raised to life eternal. The Christian's promises here are numerous, such as: "We shall be also in the likeness of his resurrection" (Rom. 6:5); "We shall also live with him" (v. 8, also 2 Tim. 2:11); "We shall also reign with him" (2 Tim. 2:12). These soul-moving promises all have their controlling *ifs,* such as: "If we have been planted together in the likeness of his death"; "If we be dead with Christ"; "If we suffer with him."

Then comes the presentation to the Father of which Paul speaks: "You . . . hath he reconciled . . . to present you holy and unblameable and unreproveable in his sight" (Col. 1:21-22). What a day that will be when the "saints come marching in"! But to do so they must have met the requirement: "If ye continue in the faith grounded and settled, and be not moved away from the hope of the gospel" (Col. 1:23).

Then come the rewards for those who have built upon the foundation "gold, silver, precious stones" (1 Cor. 3:12).

The challenge of the *ifs* can be measured only by the grandeur of the promises that follow them. Upward and onward, O my soul!

How foolish would one be in thinking that his own idea of what is best is above that of the Almighty!

Thy Will Be Done

There is no greater petition that can be made than "Thy will be done." There are those—especially some "faith healers"—that deride those who add or include this petition in their prayer when praying for healing.

In fairness to such objectors, it can be said that one could use this portion of the Lord's Prayer as an expression of fatalism—a surrender to the inevitable, an acceptance without earnest asking. There is the error expressed by James: "Ye have not, because ye ask not" (Jas. 4:2). On the other hand, to refuse to accept the principle of the divine will as best is to put oneself above God.

Why would one hesitate to say in deepest sincerity, "Thy will be done," unless he feels that what he is asking is outside the will of God? If it is not outside the divine will, then the prayer "Thy will be done" is very appropriate. One who wants the divine will done will not hesitate, but rather insist on thus praying.

One could complain of such a prayer only if he desired something outside of God's will, and only rebellious children and the devil desire anything outside the Father's will.

When one refuses to pray for the will of the Father, he must feel that his own will is superior to the Father's.

Then too, when one objects to such a prayer, he is rebelling against the plain teaching of the Master, for this is one of the main requests that He asked us to make. To do otherwise is to disobey His command.

Again it should be remembered that Jesus himself, in His bitterest struggle, abandoned His initial request, "Let this cup pass," and replaced it with "Nevertheless not my will, but thine, be done" (Luke 22:42). No one can rise higher than the Master, and He offered no prayer which would be unbecoming to any of His followers.

Some insist that the *if* should not be used in connection with a prayer for divine healing. They claim that it is God's will to heal all the sick and that the use of the *if* in this connection weakens one's faith. But no one can prove that it is God's will to heal every sick person. The Apostle Paul appears to have known more about faith healing than the "healers" of today. He did what no one under my observation has ever done and yet he relates that "Trophimus have I left at Miletum sick" (2 Tim. 4:20). And he did not invite Timothy, his son in the gospel, to a healing service but rather advised him to "drink no longer water, but use a little wine for thy stomach's sake and thine often infirmities" (1 Tim. 5:23). His advice here covers not a single spell of sickness but "thine often infirmities." He had been ailing many times and yet had not been healed.

If a person is unwilling to sincerely pray, "Thy will be done," in any and all situations, he throws himself open to bitterness when his prayer is not answered.

It is amusing (amusing if it were not so serious) to notice the reaction of one who professes that God will heal all, when no healing takes place. He immediately places the blame on others for having no faith. If he really believed that it was God's will to heal all and that such healing would come through faith—anyone's faith—why blame the lack of faith on someone else? Why didn't he do the believing himself?

God has healed in the past, and I am firm in my belief that He would like to do more for His children in this area, but I do not believe that He desires to heal all. Paul desired release from the "thorn" in his flesh, but God reminded him that His strength was made perfect in weakness and that His grace was sufficient. Whereupon, Paul said, "Most gladly therefore will I rather glory in my infirmities, that the power of Christ may rest upon me" (2 Cor. 12:9). He realized that the will of God was higher and better than his own asking. This did Christ also in the garden, and who can go beyond Paul and the Christ? Only the devil desires to do so, and such as he may mislead.

Just take a rational look at the matter. How foolish would one be in thinking that his own idea of what is best is above that of the Almighty! Such folly smacks of blasphemy.

The devil approached Eve with the "Hath God said?" question and suggested a "better" course. She took his bait and persuaded Adam to do so too. As a result, "all have sinned" and "the whole world lieth in wickedness."

It should be shouted from every housetop, included in every prayer: "Thy will be done." If it be Thy will, let it be; and if not, let it not be. The *if* is no hindrance.

The sufferings of Job and the death of Stephen reflect better the nature and the glory of God than health and deliverance from the angry mob. Paul recognized this and cried out in exultation, "That . . . Christ may be magnified in my body, whether . . . by life, or by death" (Phil. 1:20). It was God's will that he desired and not his personal health or life.

"If it be Thy will"—let this be the theme of all our asking—the deepest desire of our dedicated souls. Shun those who will not thus limit their asking. Challenge them in their error. Dethrone as usurpers of the Father's throne those who would advocate a better course than the Al-

24

mighty could devise. Submit every desire—every request—to the final test and say, "I ask this only if it be Thy will; otherwise, I ask it not." This is Christlikeness.

An untested faith could not be counted upon to call rain from a cloudless sky or fire from the heavens.

When the Brook Dries Up

The first mention of Elijah is in the first verse of the seventeenth chapter of First Kings. There he was delivering a message to Ahab, the king of Israel: "As the Lord God of Israel liveth, before whom I stand, there shall not be dew nor rain these years, but according to my word." That was a drastic message and the messenger needed protection. God provided it. He said to Elijah, "Get thee hence, and turn thee eastward, and hide thyself by the brook Cherith, that is before Jordan." The prophet obeyed and hid well; for later when Obadiah, Ahab's servant, met him, he informed Elijah that the king had sought him in every nation and found him not. He had done a good job in hiding.

It should be held in mind that Elijah was dealing with Israel's most wicked king. "Ahab did more to provoke the Lord God of Israel to anger than all the kings of Israel that were before him" (1 Kings 16:33). To deal with such a king, God used special methods.

For all we know, this was the first command that God had given to Elijah for anybody. Doubtless, God was testing him in obedience and in faith. He was to do great things in the future at the command of God and he must learn obedience. "Get thee hence . . . and hide." That was quite a command—to leave his native environment and hide from all of Israel. What would he do? How would he live? This part was to be provided; for God told him, when He ordered him to "get," that "thou shalt drink of the brook; and I have commanded the ravens to feed thee there." Elijah had to believe that promise to venture forth with peace of mind. God made good His promise. Elijah had water all the time and "bread and flesh in the morning, and bread and flesh in the evening."

He must have been by the brook for some time—time enough to meditate on the strange message from God that he gave to the king. Satan must often have reminded the prophet of the foolishness of such talk and the consequences if it did not come to pass, for in those days a prophet's life was to be taken if he prophesied in the name of the Lord and it was not fulfilled. In this case, the message was given to no mean person but to the king himself.

To add to the strength of the devil's tempting power, Elijah left word with the king that "there shall not be dew nor rain these years, but according to my word." This must have been an oft recurring trial to the prophet's faith. Just to think that he had taken upon himself the responsibility of sending rain! What if it had been the devil deceiving him all the time? What if this were a mere figment of his imagination? What if . . . ? What if . . . ? That sounds like the devil. We've all heard it before.

One source of assurance that it was God was the bread and flesh in the morning and evening, as had been promised. How could it *not* be God that had made this promise? Food by miracle could come only from God. That must have been strength for his faith. But even more wonderful, there was water—water when the whole country was dry and the king was looking in every valley and crevice for enough to sustain his family and his flocks. At least Elijah was safe. He had bread, meat, and water. What more could a man want in a famine?

But alas! Horror of horrors! The brook dried up! Water is absolutely necessary, and it was gone. Perhaps the greatest test of his faith was the fact that God had sent him to the brook. He had promised him water. Had the promise of God failed? Or was it God in the first place? Or if it were God in the beginning, had Elijah grieved Him so that His promise had failed? I will check with Elijah when I see him on the other side, but in the meantime I feel very confident that this is about the way it was. The brook had failed. The gift of God had slipped away. Does God give like that? Does He make a promise and then withdraw it? Why? Oh, why? These must have been the questions. They are timeworn and oft used by the tempter.

Why did the brook dry up? That is a good question, and I am not sure of the answer. In fact, I do not know that I need to know. I am not Elijah and that was not my brook. However, I have had brooks of my own. There may be a common cause here.

We know that faith must be tested. As the brook weakened in its flow and its stagnant pools sank into the sand, did the prophet's faith sag and sink too? I dare say that it did. An untested faith could not be counted upon to call rain from a cloudless sky or fire from the heavens. His must be strengthened. He must learn that his faith must not rest in brooks, even though God-given, but in the God that made the brook and other things as well. His security must not be in the brook but in the voice of God. Hundreds of years later Jesus announced this truth to Satan, saying, "Man shall not live by bread alone, but by every word that proceedeth out of the mouth of God."

The brook which was drying up had been located by the word of God; now another word was forthcoming—a word from the same One who had issued the first word. The brook was dry, but the God of the brook was not. He had other plans. The prophet was now to have not only food and water, but a home and fellowship. Besides that, he was to care for others—a widow and her son.

Why was he sent to the home of the widow? Jesus

commented on this in His day, saying, "Many widows were in Israel in the days of Elias," but he was sent to only one. God evidently had something in mind for Elijah. He was to see new miracles and thereby gain strength to meet the 450 false prophets, wicked Ahab, and horrible Jezebel.

Whatever may have been the thought of God in allowing the brook to dry up, of this we are sure—He had something better planned for the prophet. If this be His policy, who should care if the brook does go dry? Let it go. God has something better. Would one lament the loss of a worn-out suit if it was being replaced by a new and better one, free of charge? The tears over the drying brook are really coming from a lack of faith in a providing God. Why weep when getting something better?

God had told Elijah to go hide. If this brook had kept running, without doubt Ahab or his men would have found it and, with it, the prophet. His safety may have been in the drying of the brook. Who knows? This we do know, God will provide; and when He provides in strange and unusual or miraculous ways, our faith is thereby increased. So let Him work out His mysteries to the building of our faith and love for Him.

What is the central lesson in this story for us? It is a lesson in life's supreme and most important matter—that of obedience. Elijah obeyed. He delivered the unpopular message. He went and hid when and where he was told. Later he went to the widow's house and found it as God told him he would. He listened to God and did what He told him to do and succeeded.

Later the Lord told him to "go, shew thyself unto Ahab; and I will send rain upon the earth" (1 Kings 18:1). Because he had obeyed, he could now believe, and rain came. He listened again and obeyed, and fire came down upon his sacrifice, to the consternation of the 450 false prophets. In his prayer lay the secret, for he said, "I have done all these things at thy word."

Obedience was the secret of Elijah's successful career. That was the secret of Christ's success and the success of every other successful man of any age. "Behold, to obey is better than sacrifice, and to hearken than the fat of rams" (1 Sam. 15:22). God does not promise to give us brooks that will not go dry, but He does promise that when and if they do dry up He has another plan. Job is another illustration of the divine giving and the divine taking away, climaxing with the graciousness of the Lord in returning double for all that was taken.

There is reason to rejoice at whatever is happening in our lives if we are in the stream of absolute obedience. It is so easy for us to begin to believe in the brooks instead of in the God of the brooks. In such time, God does in mercy remove the brooks that we may turn back to Him who provided the brook in the first place. He can cause the brook to run anew, give another, or provide something better. He is a Person and not a pattern. Your brook may be different. It may never run dry. "The barrel of meal wasted not, neither did the cruse of oil fail." You may have a barrel and cruse—not a brook.

Jesus appealed for personal participation.
He never expected family unity.

"I Came... to Send... a Sword"

Hundreds of years before the Babe was born in Bethlehem who was destined to divide the human race into two classes in time (and at the end of time to place the stamp of eternity upon His classification), an ancient prophet sang of His coming and called Him "the Prince of Peace." To further emphasize His purpose and power, he declared, "Of the increase of 'iis government and peace there shall be no end" (Isa. 9:7).

The prophecy of the seer was confirmed by the song of the angelic host that announced His coming into the world. Peace was the theme of their song as they sang, "Glory to God in the highest, and on earth peace, good will toward men" (Luke 2:14).

When He would reach the hour of His ministry, what would one expect to be the theme of His message? Would it not be peace? The inspired prophet and the angelic host could not be wrong. His message, then, would be one of peace. Any other message would be inconsistent. At least so it would appear. But just listen to His message—a message so clear and unambiguous that it could not be misunderstood: "Think not that I am come to send peace on earth: I came not to send peace, but a sword" (Matt. 10:34).

Is this an impostor speaking? Has the prophet's script been altered? Have the angels changed the theme of their song? Could it be that the "Prince" has become unbalanced by His strenuous toil and all-night vigils? Some thought so, and did not hesitate to say, "He is beside himself." Others just listened and wondered, while others waited for Him to clarify His seemingly rash statement.

He did. He made it even more clear as He continued, "For I am come to set a man at variance against his father, and the daughter against her mother, and the daughter in law against her mother in law. And a man's foes shall be they of his own household" (Matt. 10:35-36).

As the Speaker continued to expound His purpose, the terms of discipleship grew more demanding. They left nothing undedicated—not even one's own life. At the close of His address, it was evident that He was not proposing a cheap "me-too," family-style religion—"I will follow because my husband wants me to," or, "Dad and Mother have gone forward; so will I." He singled the individual out and placed him on one side, and Mother, Dad, wife, husband, and/or all others on the other side. Then He said to the would-be follower: If you are to follow Me, you must turn your back on all these. If one or more of them, or even all of them, decide to follow, each in his own right, good and well. But if they all should decide to go in the other direction, you are to follow Me. If you are not willing to come on these terms, "ye cannot be my disciple."

Jesus appealed for personal participation. He never expected family unity. Should it come, it would be wonderful, but it could come only on a personal basis. Lest there might be some misunderstanding, the Master spelled the matter out in no uncertain terms: "Suppose ye that I am come to give peace on earth? I tell you, Nay; but rather division: for from henceforth there shall be five in one house divided, three against two, and two against three. The father shall be divided against the son, and the son against the father; the mother against the daughter, and the daughter against the mother; the mother in law against her daughter in law, and the daughter in law against her mother in law" (Luke 12:51-53).

There could be no question as to His terms. They were drastic, of universal application, and final. He had come to divide. His sword was in His hand and He intended to use it.

Charging the individual with final and determinate decision concerning his eternal destiny, He relieved all others of the responsibility as well as the possibility of casting the final vote for the destiny of any soul. His final commission to all of His followers laid certain very definite responsibilities upon them as He sent them forth to plead with men, in His stead, "Be ye reconciled to God." Whether His servants fulfilled this commission perfectly or ignored it completely, each individual must bear his own guilt in the day of judgment, for he will be judged by the light that he has received from the "Light, which lighteth every man that cometh into the world" (John 1:9).

By way of parenthesis, it should be said that one's eternal destiny will not be determined by the number that he presumably led to Christ, nor his fidelity in witnessing for the Saviour. Any negligence at this point will affect his reward, but his salvation will depend upon his faith in the Saviour for his own personal salvation. It is written, "They that be wise shall shine as the brightness of the firmament; and they that turn many to righteousness as the stars for ever and ever" (Dan. 12:3). It is also written, "But whosoever shall deny me before men, him will I also deny before my Father which is in heaven" (Matt. 10:33). To confess Him is to be honored; to deny Him is to be denied. One may spend all his Christian life erecting his house with "wood, hay, stubble" and be saved in the end, "yet so as by fire."

Jesus did not charge the parents to see that all their

family followed Him. To charge them with that responsibility would be to deny His statement of the divided family. And more than that, it would be charging them with a responsibility that His Heavenly Father was unable to discharge. He lost a third of the angels from heaven, and justice cannot charge His account with that loss.

The solemn and sobering conclusion is that as Christians we should do all that we can, in every way that we know to be best, to win our loved ones to discipleship. But should we gain heaven ourselves, even though one or more —even all—of our loved ones be lost, we are assured that there will be neither sorrow nor even knowledge of it there. Two clear statements from God's Word assure us of that: "And God shall wipe away all tears from their eyes; and there shall be . . . neither sorrow, nor crying, neither shall there be any more pain: for the former things are passed away" (Rev. 21:4). "Behold, I create new heavens and a new earth: and the former shall not be remembered, nor come into mind" (Isa. 65:17).

Without denying or seeking to alter what Jesus had to say about bringing a sword and division, the fact remains that He is "the Prince of Peace." Although He did affirm that He came not to bring peace but a sword upon earth, just a few days before He went back to the Father He said to His followers, "Peace I leave with you, my peace I give unto you" (John 14:27).

There is no contradiction in these seemingly contradictory statements. Jesus was speaking of peace in one group of individuals and a lack of it in another type. We should know just what He was talking about when He speaks of peace and the sword. When He talks about division and unity, they are both in His thinking and each has its place. In the four words involved, there are represented two different classes of people and two different kingdoms. "Great peace have they which love thy law"

34

(Ps. 119:165). "There is no peace, saith my God, to the wicked" (Isa. 57:21). These two statements represent two classes of people—one with peace, and the other with none. "The kingdom of God is . . . peace . . . in the Holy Ghost" (Rom. 14:17). "And the fifth angel poured out his vial upon the seat of the beast; and his kingdom was full of darkness; and they gnawed their tongues for pain" (Rev. 16:10). Here are two kingdoms—one of peace and the other of gnawing anguish.

The promises of peace so often promised by the prophets and reaffirmed by Jesus were never made to those outside of Him. And the Kingdom of peace of which He speaks is not the kingdom of this world but the one that He has gone to receive. Let no one think that the kingdom of Christ is going to be set up on this earth in this age. The lion will lie down with the lamb, and nothing will hurt nor destroy in all His holy mount. That He has promised, and that will surely come, but it will not come under the present rulers of this world nor any that will follow them. This age is going down in darkness, lawlessness, and sin. "The elements shall melt with fervent heat" and the heavens will be rolled back like a scroll before the new heaven and the new earth will appear.

God has given us a vision of the new earth with its new King, but it is folly for us to think that it will be set up by any earthly monarch. The Christian's task is not to try to make an Edenic garden out of this present earth, but to have the King enthroned in his own heart and to secure as many followers for the King as possible. In the end there will be "new heavens and a new earth, wherein dwelleth righteousness," and all that have the Kingdom established in them will be citizens of that new Kingdom. Christ, the King of Kings and Lord of Lords, will be in charge.

One should do all that he can to ease the suffering

of the helpless, minister to the needy, and do good to all men while at the same time he looks for "new heavens and a new earth, wherein dwelleth righteousness."

The devil—"the prince of the power of the air"—is the ruler of our age—"the god of this world." The kingdom of God which is within you is being organized within the territory of the enemy; hence the division and the sword.

If the shout of the saint is to be most meaningful, it must be heard other than in the camp meeting and the Sunday morning service.

When Do You Shout?

Shouting is common. When we enlarge the concept to include rejoicing, jubilation, ecstasy, as well as praises to God, we include almost all normal Christians in the category of shouters. The question of our theme is not, *Do* you shout? Most do. The real question is, *When* do you shout?

Saints and sinners have many things in common. We breathe the same air, drink the same water, eat the same food, receive the same sunshine and rain, and face the same vicissitudes of life. We have much shouting in common. When the sun is bright and the days are balmy during the vacation season, there is rejoicing from most people. When employment is high, wages good, and dividends increasing, rejoicing is general from both saint and sinner. When the wife is well and the children hale and hardy, fathers are generally happy. In short, when all goes well in the realm of the temporal, there is generally shouting. There are exceptions, but this is the rule.

In all of the occasions and circumstances enumerated above it is difficult to distinguish the saint from the sinner. The clearest light of God is not seen. The sun is too bright. The missing oil is not discovered. The Christian has but a secondary opportunity to give the Christian shout. Days must be darker for that. If the shout of the saint is to be most meaningful, it must be heard other than in the camp meeting and the Sunday morning service. If the Christian shout is to be most meaningful, it must be heard under

37

circumstances where the sinner's shout does not appear.

God has pointed out some places where the saint's shout can be most meaningful. Let us note some of them and ask ourselves if we care to be placed under the circumstances most conducive to producing the truly Christian shout.

The writer to the Hebrews points out one such place. To the harassed Hebrew saints, he wrote, "Ye . . . took joyfully the spoiling of your goods" (Heb. 10:34). The Hebrews of that day, like the Hebrews of many days and in many countries, were looked upon as being "open territory"—to be overrun by any passing army, despoiled by the robber, or destroyed in the name of God. The Hebrews thus addressed, who had become Christians, were being subjected to some such treatment. The vans were backing up to their doors and loading in anything that the marauder might deem of value to himself or whose removal might cause suffering to the new Christians.

This was a wonderful opportunity to demonstrate the true Christian shout. The shouts of prosperous, sunny days had been so mingled with the shouts of the sinners that their real nature and identity were lost. Here the Christians could exhibit without confusion the genuine joy peculiar to the person who has his affections set on things above and not on the things of this world. They took their calamity "joyfully." Joy on such occasions was distinctly Christian. They had no joiners from the world. They stood alone with their torch brightly burning where the lights of shouting from the non-Christian had dimmed or died.

The writer would not have commended the Hebrew Christians for something that was untrue. He clearly stated that they "took joyfully" the spoiling of their goods. It is interesting to note the why and the how of this. It was a unique response. In fact, their joy was "not of this world." It had come from a higher source. Their secret is given in the text: They knew in themselves "that ye have in heaven a better and an enduring substance" (Heb. 10: 34). The secret of their joy was that their true possessions were not taken from them when the heavily loaded truck with their household goods pulled away.

They may have thought, Now our beds are gone and for the first time in our lives we can unite with our Master, who had no place to lay His head. At that thought, new hallelujahs echoed through the empty rooms of their humble homes. Their hearts had been set on the "enduring substance." They remembered that their Master had said of such, "Thieves cannot break through and steal" from the place that He has gone to prepare for His own. These saints demonstrated the only recipe for shouting under adverse circumstances that is known to man. And it is known only to the saint. Here his shout stands out in bold relief against the normal attitude of the sinner and even that of the "nominal" Christian under similar conditions. God gives such opportunities to some, and when they are embraced, Christ is exalted. The world sees the evidence that the wonderful grace of God is known only to and experienced by the true saint of God.

Paul and Silas had an opportune time and a logical place to sing and shout and they had the dedication that enabled them to do it. The jail was the background. Their shout of praise was the convicting power and a whole family received Christ. In the process, they got out of jail to be on their way to another such opportunity.

Paul was able to shout, for the passion of his soul was to get the saving gospel to men, and he saw that "the things which happened unto me have fallen out rather unto the furtherance of the gospel" (Phil. 1:12). He saw that the brethren were "waxing confident by my bonds, [and] are much more bold to speak the word without fear." When he saw that through his afflictions God's strength was "made perfect in weakness," he proclaimed, "Most gladly therefore will I glory in my infirmities. . . . I take pleasure in infirmities, in reproaches, in necessities, in persecutions, in distresses for Christ's sake" (2 Cor. 12:9-10). Here the apostle waved his banner and gave his shout.

Still another place for the shout is mentioned by James: "My brethren, count it all joy when ye fall into divers temptations" (1:2). Such an hour is usually the occasion of much complaint; but not so, says James. It is the occasion for great joy. This is strange but it must be true; an apostle under the inspiration of the Holy Spirit gave this injunction to us. It is commanded, so it must be possible, the usual conduct of the professed saint notwithstanding. The path is dark here and a light is needed. Here the Christian is to let the light shine—that light that only the saint can have. Here appears the difference between the true saint and the sinner.

One need not chide himself for the lack of opportunity to manifest such joy under these circumstances mentioned above. We have not all been in jail nor seen the van moving out with our goods, so we have been denied the privilege of showing our joy at such times. But somewhere along the line, if less dramatic, we have or may have a chance to react in joy under circumstances which evoke an altogether different spirit from others.

The supreme chance to shout at a time impossible with the sinner is in the closing moments of time. Jesus depicts these moments and tells us what to do. He says, "Nation shall rise against nation, and kingdom against kingdom: and there shall be famines, and pestilences, and earthquakes in divers places. . . . Then shall they deliver you up to be afflicted, and shall kill you: and ye shall be hated of all nations for my name's sake" (Matt. 24:7-9). In describing these conditions in another address He said, "And when these things begin to come to pass, then look up, and lift up your heads; for your redemption draweth nigh" (Luke 21:28).

It should not be forgotten that the basis of the rejoicing of the Christian is in the hope and assurance of life beyond. It is the certainty of the eternal that makes such joy a shouting reality. One of the rewards that comes to us in time is the ability to shout in times like these, and such is the case only with those who have majored on the beyond. The knowledge that nothing that can befall us here can destroy us gives grounds for rejoicing.

The consciousness that our sufferings are for Christ's sake makes the shout one of "joy unspeakable and full of glory." Perhaps the weakness of our shout in the times of trouble is because we are not sure the trouble has come for Christ's sake. There is no basis for shouting for our sins, our blunders, or our self-imposed griefs. Only when it is for *His* sake that we suffer may we have this ecstasy of Christian joy.

If the world could see in the Christian more of such unexplainable shouting, would it not be constrained to get acquainted with Him who alone is the Source of it?

One looks upon the suffering Lamb of God in vain until he is able to see himself as the rightful sufferer.

"By Himself Purged Our Sins"

The songwriter rendered us a great and valuable service when he set to music those deep and meaningful words concerning our Lord:

But none of the ransomed ever knew
How deep were the waters crossed,
Nor how dark was the night that the Lord passed
through
Ere He found His sheep that was lost.

We read with amazement and with shame the record of His total desertion by His closest friends and most ardent followers. Loyalty unto death had been vehemently pledged, but alas! when the crucial hour came, "they all forsook him, and fled."

God's knowledge of the universal weakness of mankind and his inability to withstand the supreme pressure of total darkness that must surround the dying Lamb caused Him to say in advance, "I will smite the shepherd, and the sheep shall be scattered" (Mark 14:27). The inner enabling of the indwelling Holy Spirit was not theirs, for "the Holy Ghost was not yet given; because that Jesus was not yet glorified" (John 7:39). Without that enablement, they were fearful and fled.

As strange as it may seem that "all" would forsake Him, stranger still is the fact that no protecting angel hovered over Him. They had come to His aid in less crucial hours, but in this dread moment He must be "by himself" (Heb. 1:3). As Isaiah puts it, He was "cut off," as a limb from a tree, to drop into the regions of death and of hell. Separation—total and complete—must be the fate of the sinner, and the sinner's Substitute could not shun the sinner's fate and pay the price for his sins. There must be the withdrawal of the erstwhile devoted family, friends, and disciples, and the aloofness of all ministering angels. He must die alone, bereft of earthly companionship and the protection of angelic legions. The nadir of darkness had arrived. The passage could receive but one entrant— He must enter alone.

It is utterly impossible for the human mind, however strong, to measure the darkness of this dread hour. He had drained from the cup the last bitter dregs of the collective sins of mankind and having cried, "It is finished," plunged helplessly into the vortex of eternal darkness—himself alone.

This gory scene was made more tragic by a suffering more excruciating than the desertion of all earthly friends and ministering angels. It was the supreme desertion— the forsaking by the Father. Christ might understand the weakness of men and even the frailties of angels (they were all created beings), but the desertion by the Infinite wrung from Him the bitter cry, "My God, my God, why hast thou forsaken me?" He was not asking God if He had forsaken Him—that He knew. He was only asking the why of the act. With the question fresh spoken, He yielded His spirit back to God to await the answer in eternity.

This Calvary scene will bear no worthwhile meaning for us unless we understand the necessity for it. If man was to be redeemed, such an hour was inescapable. It was for the purging of our sins that this redemptive act took place.

One looks upon the suffering Lamb of God in vain until he is able to see himself as the rightful sufferer. It was not the Christ that needed to die for himself, but it was you and me for whom such suffering was just.

Sin—universal in man's nature—had necessitated a threefold punishment: physical death, separation from God, and suffering in hell. Until one accepts this punishment as just for himself, he will not accept oneness with Christ in this ordeal of threefold suffering; and until he unites with Christ in this suffering, he cannot be raised with Christ into life. "So many of us as were baptized into Jesus Christ were baptized into his death" (Rom. 6:3). "For if we have been planted together in the likeness of his death, we shall be also in the likeness of his resurrection" (Rom. 6:5).

This frightening scene on Calvary was made necessary not alone for the sins of lying, stealing, murder, and adultery. True, those who commit such crimes will suffer eternal punishment unless they repent; but every person who has reached the age of accountability deserves such punishment, even if he has committed no grossly immoral acts. Sin—the sin that made hell a necessity in the beginning—was not outward but inward. It was a state of rebellion against God—a desire to have one's own way. This is the sin of the ages and the sin of heaven that made hell necessary.

Since all have this nature of sin within, and since that is the cause of hell's creation, all men unredeemed must be lost. The awesomeness of Calvary is that since Christ, "who knew no sin," was "made . . . sin for us," His suffering was just. Until we see that, we will not repent; and without repentance, there is no salvation.

The Man Christ Jesus—unaccompanied by His friends, the angels, or His Father—must purge our sins. This He did alone. We may justly sing, "Jesus paid it all; all to Him I owe"—for "by himself [He] purged our sins."

This purging must be made by blood, for "without shedding of blood is no remission" of sins, and the Father had no blood to shed. Jesus said, "God is a Spirit" and, "A spirit hath not flesh and bones, as ye see me have" (Luke 24:39).

This purging must be made by death; hence, angels could not enter the field, for Christ was made lower than the angels for the purpose of death, for they could not die. No man could enter into this redemptive death, for the Paschal Lamb must be perfect; and since "all have sinned," humans were disqualified.

The stark necessity looms clearly before us—He must "by himself" purge "our sins."

*To be an effective Christian, one must of necessity
be acquainted with the voice of the Spirit.*

The Necessity
of Two Witnesses

It was an established rule in Old Testament days that
"in the mouth of two or three witnesses every word may
be established" (Matt. 18:16). A man could not be put to
death legally unless there were at least two witnesses
against him (cf. Num. 35:30). This was a very significant
law and with deep meaning. It has been carried over to
New Testament days and application is made of it in the
spiritual realm.

To be assured of a right relationship with God, we
need to have two witnesses. We must have the witness
of our own conscience and the witness of the Holy Spirit.
Paul brings this matter out very forcefully while comment-
ing on men's judgment of him. He adds, "I judge not mine
own self. For I know nothing against myself [margin]; yet
am I not hereby justified: but he that judgeth me is the
Lord" (1 Cor. 4:3-4).

Paul knew that he could not depend on his own conscience, for he remembered the time when with clear conscience he was killing God's children. We are told that
the time is coming when men will kill you, thinking that
they do God service (cf. John 16:2). In addition to one's
own witness, one must have the judgment of God. We have
the promise of just such a witness: "The Spirit itself
beareth witness with our spirit, that we are the children of
God" (Rom. 8:16). Our spirit and God's Spirit are two

separate and distinct entities and we must have the proof of both that we belong to God. Thank God, both are available if we are really His.

When we talk of the witness of the Spirit, we are stating our belief in a speaking God. How can He witness to us if He is silent? The whole structure of Christianity is built on the premise that there is a living, communicating God who speaks a language that a person can understand and know that it is His.

Since Jesus was made in all points like unto His brethren, His life came under the same rules that govern ours. He always kept in the love of God, but He did it by the same method that we must use to be kept in His love. This is what He said, "If ye keep my commandments, ye shall abide in my love; even as I have kept my Father's commandments, and abide in his love" (John 15:10).

The same was true of the rule of requiring two witnesses. This rule applied to Him also and He frankly admitted it. He said, "If I bear witness of myself, my witness is not true" (John 5:31). When we realize that Jesus was the only begotten Son of God, such a statement as this is difficult to understand, but He made it and it has to be true. It can be understood by us only in the context that He was truly the Son of Man and made like unto us. He had to follow the same laws of obedience, seek and obtain help from the Father, and live by Him, just as we must. Jesus was quick to add, "There is another that beareth witness of me; and I know that the witness which he witnesseth of me is true" (v. 32).

If neither Jesus nor Paul would rely upon their own testimony of themselves, how much more do I need a supporting witness! This matter is brought under further consideration by Paul. He speaks first of our spirit crying, "Abba, Father" (Rom. 8:15). This is the cry of the soul which has received "the Spirit of adoption." It is the Christian's spirit calling God, "Father." Isn't that enough—an adopted child calling God, "Father"? Is that not dependable? No, it is not enough. Is a child of God, having received the Spirit of adoption, better than the only begotten Son of God? Yet the Son would not rely upon His own witness concerning himself. He required and obtained a higher witness—the witness of the Father. How dare we think that we can get by with less?

The Apostle Paul tells us of another Spirit within us crying, "Abba, Father." This, too, is based upon our sonship: "And because ye are sons, God hath sent forth the Spirit of his Son into your hearts, crying, Abba, Father" (Gal. 4:6). So here we have it—two spirits crying the same thing—ours and His. Thus the requirement of the two witnesses is met and we are accepted with God by the witness of our own conscience attested by the Spirit of God.

This principle of the double check must be followed in ascertaining the will of God. Jesus brought a second word to bear on the quotation used by Satan and changed the matter completely. We too are asked to compare "spiritual things with spiritual," so as to come to the full understanding of the Father's will for us. Following this divinely announced pattern, we are thrown wholly upon God for the assurance of our relationship with Him. The conscience could be warped and defiled and thus be utterly unreliable; therefore it cannot be the final proof that I am right with God. God will not validate the testimony of my conscience if it is false. Yet one needs the voice of his own conscience, lest he be led astray by the devil under the deceitful guise of the divine voice. One cannot be right if his conscience condemns him.

The thrill of the testimony of the two witnesses—mine and God's—is wonderful indeed. This is the reason Paul could say, "But with me it is a very small thing that I should be judged of you, or of man's judgment" (1 Cor.

48

4:3). If my own redeemed soul witnesses that God is my Father and "the Spirit itself" bears the same witness, why should I care what anyone thinks? The combined opinion of all men, angels, and demons would be meaningless as against God and me; for "if God be for us, who can be against us?" (Rom. 8:31). Here lies the secret of a happy and victorious life; and if one hasn't found it, he should examine himself and see if he "be in the faith."

From other teachings of Jesus we see how necessary it is to have the two witnesses. He tells us of the multitude that will come to the judgment thinking that they are saved but are not. They have relied upon the witness of their own souls, their good deeds, or something else and are not ready. He said, "Not every one that saith unto me, Lord, Lord, shall enter into the kingdom of heaven" (Matt. 7:21). It is quite alarming when we know that there will be many in this class. The two witnesses are imperative.

To be an effective Christian, one must of necessity be acquainted with the voice of the Spirit. There can be no finality in the midst of uncertainty. Here we have the assurance that "my sheep know my voice." Here we are brought back to the fact that there must be an understandable relationship between man's soul and the Spirit.

When one has the known witness of the Spirit, he can then testify in full assurance and boldness. He now knows not alone by his own conscience, which could be a false guide, but from God himself. We see this illustrated in the words of Jesus. He was testifying of himself one day and the Pharisees, remembering that He had said that He could not rely upon His own witness, said to Him: "Thou bearest record of thyself; thy record is not true. Jesus answered . . . Though I bear record of myself, yet my record is true; for I know whence I came, and whither I go. . . . For I am not alone, but I and the Father that sent me" (John 8:13-16). Jesus was free to speak for himself, since

49

He had the approval and the presence of the Father. In like manner, our testimony can be bold when we have the Father's okay upon it.

What shall we say in the light of this imperative? Shall we settle for less than is essential? Shall we continue with a "form of godliness" while denying the power thereof? Shall we draw back from the voice of the witnessing Spirit because some have gone into fanaticism at this point? The correct answer to all of these questions is self-evident. The crying need of the professed Christian is to have a conscious and understandable relationship with the speaking Spirit, who witnesses to our right relationship with God. Nothing less than this can please God, nor is it safe.

If acquaintance with the speaking Spirit can be established at this point, the constant leadership of the Spirit will be less difficult to understand. When one is thus led, he has the proof of his sonship: "For as many as are led by the Spirit of God, they are the sons of God" (Rom. 8:14).

In this area, as in all others wherein we deal with God, faith is a factor. "Without faith it is impossible to please him." Here we need faith to believe that we can have a living, conscious contact with the witnessing Spirit. Whatever we get from God must come by faith, whether it is the salvation of our souls, the reception of the Holy Spirit, the witness of the Spirit, or the leadership of the Spirit. All must come by faith.

The first step on the road to faith and the Spirit's leadership is a "conscience void of offence toward God, and toward men." While the human conscience cannot be the final word in the matter, as we have already seen, nevertheless it is necessary—in fact, indispensable. One cannot be right and have a guilty conscience. This guilt must be cleared Godward and manward. When the conscience bears its witness, we are in a position to seek ratification by the witnessing Spirit. If our own conscience has not deceived us, faith will take hold of the Spirit and His witness will be had. With this we have the two witnesses necessary for full assurance of faith. This is the path of certainty and peace—the peace of God.

Forever Settled

Living as we do in a world of constant change, it is heartening to know that there is something eternally fixed; such is the Word of God. The Psalmist wrote, "For ever, O Lord, thy word is settled in heaven" (Ps. 119:89). Isaiah takes up the theme and declares, "The grass withereth, the flower fadeth: but the word of our God shall stand for ever" (40:8).

If further proof is desired, just listen to Jesus, "Heaven and earth shall pass away, but my words shall not pass away" (Matt. 24:35). Here we have an invincible, immovable, eternal foundation on which to build and abide. Eternal security is assured one who thus builds. At the conclusion of the Sermon on the Mount, Jesus affirmed that the hearer who built on His words would have a storm-proof house.

Elsewhere in the Word we are assured that "he that doeth the will of God abideth for ever" (1 John 2:17). The will of God is expressed in His Word, and His Word is unchanging. It needs no change now or hereafter, for it was perfect when announced.

Because of the fixedness and finality of God's will as expressed in His Word, Jesus realized that He could be pleasing to the Father only by adhering to His Word. He tells us, "If ye keep my commandments, ye shall abide in my love; even as I have kept my Father's commandments, and abide in his love" (John 15:10).

Thus speaking, Jesus is saying two things. He points

out the only path that He could take and retain the Father's love. Twice He announced His purpose to do this, but here He points out its indispensability if He was to retain God's love. In thus speaking, He is also pointing out the only path for us if we are to retain His love. Obedience, then, is the very essence of love. "For this is the love of God, that we keep his commandments" (1 John 5:3); and if I "have not charity [love], I am nothing" (1 Corinthians 13:2).

Without the indwelling Christ, one is not His; for "if any man have not the Spirit of Christ, he is none of his" (Rom. 8:9). Obedience is proof of His indwelling, for "he that keepeth his commandments dwelleth in him, and he in him" (1 John 3:24). At the same time, disobedience is proof that one is *not* His; for "why call ye me, Lord, Lord, and do not the things which I say?" (Luke 6:46).

The "Thy will be done in earth, as it is in heaven" (in the Lord's Prayer) is but an expressed desire that the sum total of our living have eternal value. Since His Word and will are fixed in heaven, and no discord will be allowed there, it follows that only what is done in accordance with His fixed will can be abiding. Neither man nor the works of man can live forever except as they follow the divine pattern.

Here we are faced with the temporal and the eternal, and each and every person is pursuing the one or the other. One is following his own will or else the will of the Father. Mankind divides into two classes at this point.

It is God's expressed desire that we have eternal life. For that purpose Christ came to earth. He desires that the labors of our hands have eternal value also, and for that reason He has commanded us to lay up our treasures in heaven. Heaven is fixed: its coffers cannot be raided, nor can its mansions be destroyed!

"Change and decay" are all about us, but neither can

be said of heaven. And we have been invited there! The changes of time cannot affect us if we have our hearts "fixed," trusting in the Lord. Thus fixed, we may be "stedfast, unmoveable, always abounding in the work of the Lord" (1 Cor. 15:58). This can be true because we have received a "kingdom which cannot be moved" (Heb. 12:28); and abiding in that Kingdom, we can survive the passing and inherit the eternal.

With the fixedness of our souls, the fixedness of our Kingdom, and the fixedness of our treasures, we can face life's crumbling towers and tottering mountains. We can laugh as the heavens are folded up as a worn-out mantle and cast away, knowing that our heritage is untouched.

Fixed—settled—eternally secure! What a thought! If all has been committed to the Heavenly Keeper, all will be kept against that day. Reckless joy can flood our souls and we can face the onslaughts of the evil and the evil one. In the face of seeming dissolution we can cry, "None of these things move me." We can swell the chorus, "I will not fear what man shall do unto me," remembering with Job that "my redeemer liveth . . . and though after my skin worms destroy this body, yet in my flesh shall I see God" (Job 19:25-26).

Now is the hour to sound the Christian's note of security and fixedness, for all about us men's hearts are beginning to fail. The cornerstones of their self-made mansions are sinking and the cracks are beginning to appear in the walls. Youth is roaming the untrod plains and forests, seeking paths that are not there, and parents stand helplessly by in near despair.

Against such a background of the soiled and the sordid, the vain and vanishing, the pomp and the pride of sinful men, may we raise the cry of triumph, and in the face of dissolution declare our faith in the eternal. May God help us to trim our lamps and place them on the hills, that pilots of the skies may not miss the runway.

May our shakers be filled with the salt of saving grace, and may we get to the lockers before the meat decays. To the tasks of God's designing may we march in triumph and not trepidity. May our song be dynamic and not a dirge.

Let us lift our eyes above the foam-crested waves that wildly wash our feet and see the calm and conquering Master standing in the deep.

Forgive us, Lord, for our fears, and our failures begotten by them, and renew or, if necessary, create within us a faith that knows no fear and a courage that fails us never. Then the world will see the Christ of Conquest and some will follow Him.

The ministry of suffering might be looked upon as morbid and depressing but for the fact that it is supported by joy.

Fruitful Suffering

Not all suffering is fruitful. The songwriter voices this in his lines:

> *Oh, what peace we often forfeit,*
> *Oh, what needless pain we bear,*
> *All because we do not carry*
> *Everything to God in prayer.*

The truth of these words is well anchored in the Word: "Be careful for nothing; but in every thing by prayer . . . let your requests be made known unto God. And the peace of God . . . shall keep [you]" (Phil. 4:6-7).

Having by obedience eliminated the fruitless sufferings, there remain those types of sufferings that bear rich and eternal fruit. Such sufferings may be divided into two general categories: (1) Those producing, or at least meant to produce, beneficial results in the life of the sufferer; and (2) Those which are designed to help others.

· In the first group could be mentioned the following:

Conviction for sin, which is a form of suffering, comes to produce repentance, the indispensable prerequisite to peace and pardon. Happy is the sinner who is thus called upon to suffer. It may become the door to eternal life.

There is the suffering caused by inbred sin—this internal warring with a foreign enemy whom we willingly harbor. This suffering is a painful call to deliver this man of sin—the carnal mind—to the Holy Executioner, that the soul may have peace and rest in God, which can be obtained in no other way.

There is the suffering of the Christian because of blunders, errors, and faults. This suffering is given to us for corrective purposes. In this field are the rebukes and reproofs from God's messengers, as well as the chastening of the Lord. They are given that we may be led to "confess your faults one to another" and thereby keep reconciled to God and to man. God's chastening is to enlarge the soul's capacity and to fill it with His holiness. One should rejoice in such moments of fruit-bearing sufferings.

There is the suffering that comes with normal growth or expansion pains. In youth, they are called "growing pains." They are the opening up of the personality, the enlargement of the soul, and the deepening of the Christian life. They come, not as chastening because of error, but from breaking into new territory. It is like the opening up of "new ground" for the farmer's expanding field for cultivation.

Such sufferings as the above are, in a primary sense, for the benefit of the individual sufferer. Since "none of us liveth to himself, and no man dieth to himself," there are marginal benefits accruing to the accounts of others, but the major benefits are personal.

In like manner, there are other types of suffering which, while yielding fruit in the life of the sufferer, are more especially of an altruistic nature—designed to help others, to advance the cause of the Kingdom, and to bring glory to God.

Such is the suffering for truth's sake. Paul felt the sting of such when he said, "Am I therefore become your enemy, because I tell you the truth?" Love must be "in deed and in truth," and truth is painful at times. But love will suffer the pain of whatever unfavorable reaction to the truth may come, for it is dedicated to the truth. Here the truth is the primary beneficiary.

There is suffering for Godlikeness. This is inevitable: "Because . . . I have chosen you out of the world, therefore the world hateth you" (John 15:19). Righteousness produces pain in the unrepentant sinner and it often reacts as suffering in the Christian. Here righteousness is exalted, God is honored, and the suffering saint rewarded.

There is the suffering of comradeship. "Weep with them that weep" is taught by God and was practiced by His Son while upon earth. In a common suffering the Christian bonds are strengthened and the mutual participation divides the load of sorrow with another.

There is the suffering of intercession when one feels the sinner's plight as his own and pleads for himself as the guilty. The woman from Canaan illustrates this type. Her petition was "Have mercy on me,- O Lord, thou son of David; my daughter is grievously vexed with a devil" (Matt. 15:22). She had assumed the problem as her own and made petition for herself. The prayer was rewarded.

The Holy Spirit, who "maketh intercession for us with groanings which cannot be uttered" (Rom. 8:26), represents the highest possible form of such suffering. Christ also ministered here. Isaiah tells us that "he hath borne our griefs, and carried our sorrows" (Isa. 53:4). He made our sins His own and "was wounded for our transgressions, he was bruised for our iniquities" (v. 5).

To a large degree, the Apostle Paul entered this field, declaring, "I . . . now rejoice in my sufferings for you, and fill up that which is behind of the afflictions of Christ in my flesh for his body's sake, which is the church" (Col. 1:24).

Such a ministry might be looked upon as morbid and depressing, but for the fact that it is supported by joy. Paul tells us that he rejoiced in his suffering. On another occasion, he said, "Most gladly therefore will I rather glory in my infirmities. . . . I take pleasure . . . in reproaches, in necessities, in persecutions, in distresses for Christ's sake" (2 Cor. 12:9-10).

Such suffering is creative and redemptive. It is the birth pains of new lives. Paul puts it this way: "My little children, of whom I travail in birth again until Christ be formed in you" (Gal. 4:19).

To the Thessalonians he wrote, "Ye remember . . . our labour and travail" (1 Thess. 2:9). The promise made to Jesus—"He shall see of the travail of his soul, and shall be satisfied"—will be shared by all who thus suffer. "Your labour is not in vain in the Lord" (2 Cor. 15:58).

The key to all this glorious treasure lies in our hands.
The storehouse is God's, but its key is ours.

Children of the Highest

"Ye shall be the children of the Highest" (Luke 6:35). What a thought! In fact, it is a thought so vast, so deep, so high, so wide, so all-embracing, that the human mind cannot encompass it.

It would be as impossible for one to explore and understand the full meaning of this statement of the Master as it would be for a lad to dip the Pacific Ocean dry with a thimble.

"Children of the Highest"—the "Highest," who moves the galaxies through space and holds the waters in His hand—the Creator, who bedecked the night's dark sky with scintillating stars, and spread a golden carpet for the feet of the new-made sun—the Creator, who owns the cattle on a thousand hills, and lays the carpet of grass on which they feed—the "Highest," whose scepter sways the nations and whose Word will judge all created beings.

"Ye shall be the children of the Highest"—children who will share the glory of His Son and inherit with Him all things—children upon whom the gaze of the Father is ever turned, and whose every need is the Father's constant care. Children—"heirs of God"—who are destined to reign with His Son forever. These are the promises made by the Son and they will be fulfilled by the Father.

More we could not ask—more we could never need—sonship—security—limitless resources—eternal well-being —all for which one could hope, desire, or dream! "All things are yours"; this is the promise, and thus it shall be.

The key to all this glorious treasure lies in our hands. The storehouse is God's, but its key is ours, and that key is faith. Faith must open the storehouse and only faith *can* open it; for "without faith it is impossible to please him."

The faith that opens is the faith that obeys. It is the kind of faith seen in Abraham, of whom it is said, "By faith Abraham . . . obeyed" (Heb. 11:8). No other faith but obedient faith works. And what are we to obey to warrant God's fulfillment of these promises? We need not search far nor too long to find them; they form a part of the promise itself. Note them:

"Love your enemies, do good to them which hate you."

"Bless them that curse you."

"Unto him that smiteth thee on the one cheek offer also the other."

"Him that taketh away thy cloke forbid not to take thy coat also."

"Give to every man that asketh of thee."

"Of him that taketh away thy goods ask them not again."

"Love ye your enemies, and do good, and lend, hoping for nothing again."

Then comes the promise, "Your reward shall be great, and ye shall be the children of the Highest" (Luke 6:27-35).

Volumes have been written on these words—some to explain them away—some to show that they are unattainable ideals in this life—some to show that they are guidelines for conduct in the world yet to come. Some have spiritualized them so as to render their literal fulfillment impossible. There are others, though few in number, who believe that Jesus meant these commands to be kept in this life, and that the promise based upon their obedience is to have literal fulfillment.

61

We need not write a commentary on this passage—write your own. Take the commandments one by one and examine your own attitude and practice in the light of them. These are the words of the Master; take them seriously. Be honest in the light of them. Ask yourself, Do I keep these commandments; and if occasion has not arisen that demands that they be kept, is it the purpose and the disposition of my soul to keep them if and when such occasion should arise?

If your answer is not a positive one, then remember the words of the Master: "Why call ye me, Lord, Lord, and do not the things which I say?" (Luke 6:46). And before dismissing the subject, remember that He also said, "Many will say to me in that day, Lord, Lord, have we not prophesied in thy name? and in thy name have cast out devils? and in thy name done many wonderful works? And then will I profess unto them, I never knew you: depart from me, ye that work iniquity" (Matt. 7:22-23). Would you be in that crowd? If you glibly answer, "No," then remember—neither did those who were in it think that they were included. "Examine yourselves" is the injunction of the Word.

If there is no Spirit of His Son in your heart, "crying, Abba, Father," then just draw the black drapes over the beautiful picture of His children's heritage alluded to in our opening sentences; the treasure is not for you. The message for you—your final message—will be, "I never knew you: depart from me." Forget all the miracles done in My name and all your profession of sonship with Me. If you had been heir with Me, My Spirit would have been bearing witness with your spirit. You had the wonderful works, but not the witness—you are not Mine. "Depart"—depart forever.

When one honestly faces the Sermon on the Mount and seeks to keep it, that he may obtain the oneness with

God that he desires, he must realize that faith is necessary.

Do I dare to turn the other cheek—give my "coat also" —"give to every man"—ask not for the return of taken goods? In short, am I willing to follow Him even unto death?

Whatever the answer, it can be said in truth that one cannot get below his Master, who said, "The foxes have holes, and the birds of the air have nests; but the Son of man hath not where to lay his head" (Matt. 8:20).

If one recoils from such a path, remember that He said, "The disciple is not above his master, nor the servant above his lord. It is enough for the disciple that he be as his master" (Matt. 10:24-25).

You dare not try to claim the promise unless you are willing to pay its price. He became "obedient unto death," and those who will sit with Him in His throne must love "not their lives unto the death" (Rev. 12:11).